D0647074

First Facts®

Get To Know **Reptiles**

Get to Know

KOMODO DRAGONS

by Flora Brett

CAPSTONE PRESS

a capstone imprint

First Facts are published by Capstone Press,
1710 Roe Crest Drive, North Mankato, Minnesota 56003
www.capstonepub.com

Library of Congress Cataloging-in-Publication Data
Brett, Flora, author.
Get to know Komodo dragons / by Flora Brett.
        pages cm.—(First facts. Get to know reptiles)
Summary: "Discusses Komodo dragons, including their physical
features, habitat, range, diet, and life cycle."—Provided by publisher.
Audience: Ages 6–9.
Audience: K to grade 3.
Includes bibliographical references and index.
ISBN 978-1-4914-2062-1 (library binding)
ISBN 978-1-4914-2246-5 (paperback)
ISBN 978-1-4914-2268-7 (ebook PDF)
1. Komodo dragon—Juvenile literature. 2. Komodo Island
(Indonesia)—Juvenile literature. I. Title.
QL666.L29B74 2015
597.95'968—dc23
                        2014023859

Editorial Credits
Nikki Bruno Clapper, editor; Cynthia Akiyoshi, designer; Svetlana
    Zhurkin, media researcher; Katy LaVigne, production specialist

Photo Credits
Dreamstime: Artem Furman, 17, Zuzana Randlova, cover, back cover,
1, 2, 24; Minden Pictures: Michael Pitts, 15 (bottom), Stephen Belcher,
7, Tui De Roy, 11; Newscom: Danita Delimont Photography/Tony
Berg, 20, imageBROKER/J.W.Alker, 19, Photoshot/NHPA/B. Jones
& M. Shimlock, 21; Shutterstock: Dean Bertoncelj, 13, Odua Images
(background), cover and throughout, Richard Susanto, 5, Sergey
Uryadnikov, 9 (bottom)

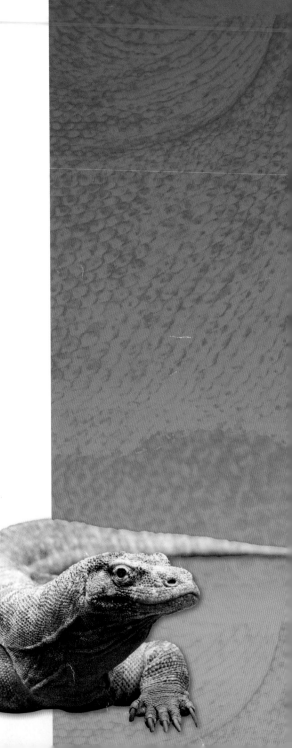

Printed in the United States of America in
North Mankato, Minnesota.
092014   008482CGS15

Table of Contents

A Giant Discovery

In the 1800s Europeans heard scary stories about faraway monsters. People said "land crocodiles" roamed Komodo Island in Indonesia. In the early 1900s European scientists went to Indonesia. They didn't find real monsters. But they did find monstrous lizards. The scientists named the lizards Komodo dragons.

These **cold-blooded reptiles** live only on five islands in Indonesia. Komodo dragons are the world's largest and heaviest lizards.

cold-blooded—having a body temperature that changes with the surrounding temperature

reptile—a cold-blooded animal that breathes air and has a backbone; most reptiles have scales

Fact:

Komodo dragons have lived on Earth for millions of years. But the Western part of the world did not know about them until 1910.

Komodo dragon in Komodo National Park, Indonesia

Short and Tough

Komodo dragons do look a bit like monsters. They can be 10 feet (3 meters) long. They weigh up to 300 pounds (136 kilograms). The lizards are covered with **scales**. Their skin is black, brown, green, or gray. The skin acts like armor to protect the lizards. Komodo dragons have long tails, short legs, and sharp claws.

These lizards have especially fearsome mouths. Forked yellow tongues flick in and out of their mouths constantly. Inside are about 60 sharp, jagged teeth.

scale—one of many small, hard pieces of skin that cover an animal's body

Komodo dragon on Rinca Island, Indonesia

Fact:

Komodo dragons are closely related to snakes. Like snakes, Komodo dragons use their tongues to smell.

Small Range, Small Numbers

Komodo dragons have a small **range**. Most Komodo dragons live on the island of Komodo, Indonesia. Others live on nearby islands. Scientists believe only around 4,000 Komodo dragons live in this small area.

Komodo dragons' small numbers make them **endangered**. Komodo National Park was formed in 1980 to help protect the lizards. Hunting Komodo dragons and their food sources is illegal in the park.

range—an area where an animal mostly lives

endangered—in danger of dying out

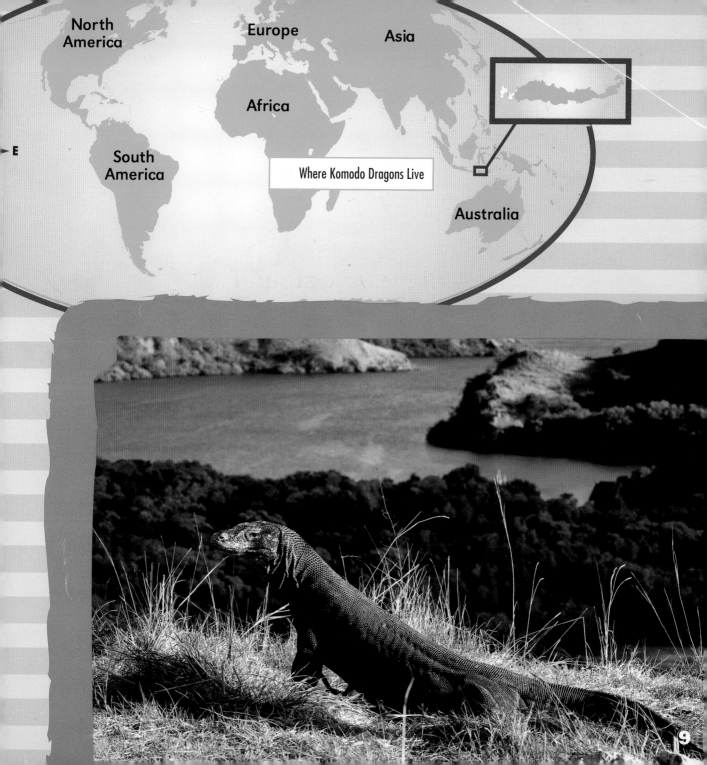

North America

Europe

Asia

Africa

South America

Where Komodo Dragons Live

Australia

E

Hot Habitats

The islands where Komodo dragons live are hilly and hot. The lizards can be found in **grasslands** and forests near beaches. Dragons dig deep **burrows** so they can keep cool in their hot **habitats**.

Adult Komodo dragons live alone. They often claim one area of land as their own. Then they attack the other Komodo dragons they see.

Fact:
Komodo dragons come together only to mate and to eat.

female Komodo dragon
protecting her burrow

grassland—a large area of wild grasses

burrow—a tunnel or hole in the ground
made or used by an animal

habitat—the natural place and conditions
in which a plant or animal lives

Dragon Dinner

Adult Komodo dragons eat deer, pigs, goats, cows, and water buffalo. The lizards hide in tall grass and watch for **prey**. Once the prey is close, they attack quickly. Komodo dragons also eat animals that are already dead.

Scientists once believed that **bacteria** in the dragon's mouth killed prey. They now know that the lizard's **venom** makes prey go into **shock**. The venom also keeps the prey's blood flowing. The blood loss causes the prey's death.

Fact:
Komodo dragons can follow a dead animal's scent from 7 miles (11 kilometers) away.

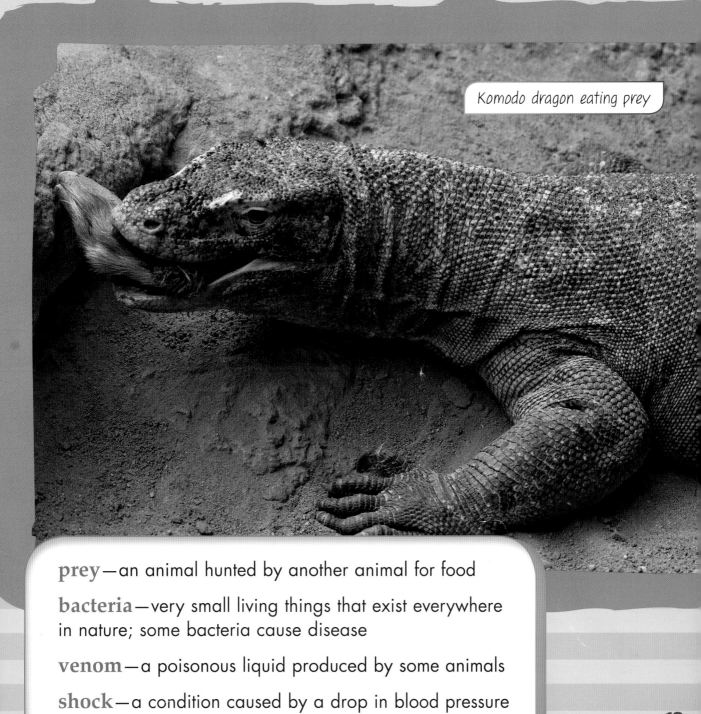

Komodo dragon eating prey

prey—an animal hunted by another animal for food

bacteria—very small living things that exist everywhere in nature; some bacteria cause disease

venom—a poisonous liquid produced by some animals

shock—a condition caused by a drop in blood pressure

Producing Young

Komodo dragons **mate** in spring and summer. Male dragons fight over females. Two males try to knock each other down. The winning dragon mates with the female.

The female digs a nest and lays 20 to 40 eggs. Then she leaves the nest. The eggs hatch in about eight months.

Komodo dragon **hatchlings** weigh only 2.5 to 3.5 ounces (71 to 99 grams). They have green skin with yellow stripes.

Fact:
A female dragon sometimes hisses after a mating fight. She wants the winner to leave.

mate—to join with another to produce young

hatchling—a young animal that has just come out of its egg

Komodo Dragon Life Cycle

A dragon hatches and becomes an adult. Then it mates and has its own babies.

Komodo dragon hatchlings

Growing Up

Few young Komodo dragons live to become adults. Adult Komodo dragons and other **predators** often eat young dragons.

Many young dragons live in trees to stay safe. They eat other small reptiles and insects that crawl along branches. Komodo dragons move to the ground when they are about 4 years old.

Fact:

Young Komodo dragons often live together. They split up when they are old enough to fight off predators.

predator—an animal that hunts other animals for food

Threats to Komodo Dragons

People are the biggest threats to Komodo dragons. People destroy dragons' habitats to build homes. Forest clearing has made the lizards' food less available.

Some tourists feed wild Komodo dragons. Then the reptiles don't learn to hunt. They starve after the tourists leave.

Fact:
Komodo dragons are not hurt by one another's venom. Scientists think that **antibodies** protect dragons from one another.

antibody—a substance in the body that fights against infection and disease

tourists watching a Komodo dragon in Komodo National Park

Protecting Komodo Dragons

Most Komodo dragons live in the protected Komodo National Park. Scientists study the dragons' mating behavior there. They also study the number of prey available to the dragons. Scientists at zoos around the world mate Komodo dragons and raise the hatchlings. These efforts will help keep Komodo dragons in the world.

Amazing but True!

Komodo dragons can eat half their body weight in less than 20 minutes. The lizard's jaw and throat muscles let it quickly swallow huge chunks. Sometimes a dragon must flee from danger after a meal. It simply throws up the food. Then the dragon can run away quickly.

Komodo dragon swallowing a wild boar

Glossary

antibody (AN-ti-bah-dee)—a substance in the body that fights against infection and disease

bacteria (back-TIHR-ee-uh)—very small living things that exist everywhere in nature; some bacteria cause disease

burrow (BUR-oh)—a tunnel or hole in the ground made or used by an animal

cold-blooded (KOHLD–BLUHD-id)—having a body temperature that changes with the surrounding temperature

endangered (en-DAYN-jurd)—in danger of dying out

grassland (GRAS-land)—a large area of wild grasses

habitat (HAB-uh-tat)—the natural place and conditions in which a plant or animal lives

hatchling (HACH-ling)—a young animal that has just come out of its egg

mate (MAYT)—to join with another to produce young

predator (PRED-uh-tur)—an animal that hunts other animals for food

prey (PRAY)—an animal hunted by another animal for food

range (RAYNJ)—an area where an animal mostly lives

reptile (REP-tile)—a cold-blooded animal that breathes air and has a backbone; most reptiles have scales

scale (SKALE)—one of many small, hard pieces of skin that cover an animal's body

shock (SHOK)—a condition caused by a drop in blood pressure

venom (VEN-uhm)—a poisonous liquid produced by some animals

Read More

Cain, Patrick G. *Komodo Dragon*. Great Predators. Minneapolis: ABDO Pub. Co., 2013.

Maimone, Max. *Hunting with Komodo Dragons*. Animal Attack! New York: Gareth Stevens Publishing, 2014.

Owings, Lisa. *The Komodo Dragon*. Pilot Books: Nature's Deadliest. Minneapolis: Bellwether Media, 2012.

Internet Sites

FactHound offers a safe, fun way to find Internet sites related to this book. All of the sites on FactHound have been researched by our staff.

Here's all you do:
Visit *www.facthound.com*
Type in this code: 9781491420621

Check out projects, games and lots more at
www.capstonekids.com

Critical Thinking Using the Common Core

1. Komodo dragons are endangered. What does this mean? (Key Ideas and Details)

2. How do Komodo dragons kill and eat their prey? Compare and contrast these habits with those of another predator. For instance, think about a bear, a spider, or an owl. (Integration of Knowledge and Ideas)

Index